W9-AQV-642

Date: 7/24/12

J 598 GRA
Gray, Susan Heinrichs.
The life cycle of birds /

PALM BEACH COUNTY
LIBRARY SYSTEM
3650 SUMMIT BLVD.
WEST PALM BEACH, FL 33406

LIFE CYCLES

# The Life Cycle of Birds

Susan H. Gray

Heinemann
LIBRARY

Chicago, Illinois

**www.heinemannraintree.com**
Visit our website to find out more information about Heinemann-Raintree books.

**To order:**

☎ Phone 888-454-2279

💻 Visit www.heinemannraintree.com to browse our catalog and order online.

© 2012 Heinemann Library
an imprint of Capstone Global Library, LLC
Chicago, Illinois

All rights reserved. No part of this publication may be reproduced or transmitted in any form or by any means, electronic or mechanical, including photocopying, recording, taping, or any information storage and retrieval system, without permission in writing from the publisher.

Edited by Abby Colich, Megan Cotugno, and Kate deVilliers
Designed by Victoria Allen
Illustrated by Darren Lingard
Picture research by Ruth Blair
Originated by Capstone Global Library, Ltd.
Printed and bound in China by CTPS

14 13 12 11
10 9 8 7 6 5 4 3 2 1

**Library of Congress Cataloging-in-Publication Data**
Gray, Susan Heinrichs.
  The life cycle of birds / Susan H. Gray.
    p. cm.—(Life cycles)
  Includes bibliographical references and index.
  ISBN 978-1-4329-4979-2 (hc)—ISBN 978-1-4329-4986-0
(pb)  1. Birds—Life cycles—Juvenile literature.  I. Title.
  QL676.2.G725 2012
  598.156—dc22                    2010038277

**Acknowledgments**
The author and publisher are grateful to the following for permission to reproduce copyright material: © Corbis: pp. 5 (© Sally A. Morgan; Ecoscene), 6 (© STRINGER/INDIA/Reuters), 14 (© David Ponton/Design Pics), 21 (© Frans Lanting), 22 (© Wayne Lynch/All Canada Photos), 23 (© Jamie Harron; Papilio), 26 (© Lynda Richardson), 30 (© Wayne Lynch/All Canada Photos), 33 (© Brooklyn Museum), 45 (© Neil Farrin/JAI); © Photolibrary: p. 27 (OSF/Sven Zacek); © Science Photo Library: p. 19 (Steve Gschmeissner); © Shutterstock: pp. 4 (© Al Mueller), 7 (© jaludwig), 8 (© Brandon Seidel), 11 (© Near and Far Photography), 12 (© Denis Tabler), 15 (© Anastasija Popova), 16 (© mlorenz), 17 (© Cheryl E. Davis), 18 (© Johan Swanepoel), 20 (© Mogens Trolle), 24 (© Steve Heap), 25 (© RazvanZinica), 28 (© Roseanne Smith), 29 (© pix2go), 31 (© Dennis Donohue), 32 (© Chesapeake Images), 34 (© godrick), 35 (© Dennis Donohue), 36 (© Alexander Yu. Zotov), 38 (© S.Cooper Digital), 39 (© PozitivStudija), 40 (© MindStorm), 41 (© Karel Gallas).

Cover photograph reproduced with permission from © Getty Images (Minden Pictures/Mitsuaki Iwago).

We would like to thank Dr. Michael Bright for his invaluable help in the preparation of this book.

Every effort has been made to contact copyright holders of any material reproduced in this book. Any omissions will be rectified in subsequent printings if notice is given to the publisher.

**Disclaimer**
All the Internet addresses (URLs) given in this book were valid at the time of going to press. However, due to the dynamic nature of the Internet, some addresses may have changed, or sites may have changed or ceased to exist since publication. While the author and publisher regret any inconvenience this may cause readers, no responsibility for any such changes can be accepted by either the author or the publisher.

# Contents

Some words are shown in bold, **like this**. You can find out what they mean by looking in the glossary.

**Look but don't touch:** Many birds are easily hurt. If you see one in the wild, do not get too close to it. Look at it, but do not try to touch it!

# What Is a Bird?

Birds are animals that have wings covered with feathers. Most are excellent fliers. Birds also have hard bills, or beaks, that they use to get food. Most have sharp eyesight. They can spot their food at great distances. Some, such as owls, can even see it in the dark.

## Vertebrates

Birds are **vertebrates**. A vertebrate is an animal with a backbone that helps to support its body. Birds are also warm-blooded. The body temperature of a warm-blooded animal always stays about the same. It does not drop on cold days or rise on warm days. A bird's normal body temperature is just a little warmer than a human's.

By beating its wings more than 40 times a second, this tiny hummingbird seems to hang in midair.

Birds lay eggs with hard shells. Babies grow inside the eggs, using up the food that surrounds them. Before they lay eggs, most birds prepare nests. Some make very complex nests, while others simply find a place that seems safe.

**The Early Bird**
About 150 years ago, a man in Germany made an unusual discovery. He found a **fossil** of a strange bird. The bird had wings and feathers, but it also looked like a small dinosaur. It had died millions of years ago. The bird was given the name *Archaeopteryx* which means **ancient** wing. Many scientists believe it was one of the earliest birds ever to exist on Earth.

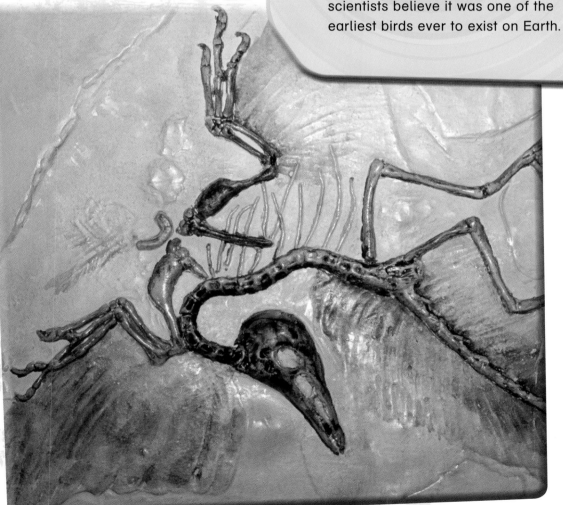

# What Are the Different Kinds of Birds?

People have discovered and named almost 10,000 different **species**, or kinds, of birds. There are probably many more that have not yet been discovered. But with this many kinds of birds, how do scientists sort them all out? They use a special **classification** system. It involves organizing the birds into different groups.

This rare bird was discovered in India in 1995. Scientists believe that many birds have not yet been discovered.

# Classifying birds

This is how classification works. All birds fit into a huge group of living things called animals. This enormous group is called a kingdom. Scientists divide the animal kingdom into many other groups. Each one of these groups is called a **phylum**. So there is a phylum that includes jellyfish, a phylum just for earthworms, a phylum for spiders and insects, and so on. Birds fit into a phylum that also includes mammals, fish, reptiles, and amphibians.

Scientists further divide each phylum into classes. The class that includes all of the birds is called **Aves**. This comes from the Latin word for bird.

**Forever Changing**

Years ago, scientists divided all living things into two kingdoms—the animal kingdom and the plant kingdom. But over time, they learned more about all the different kinds of living things. They saw that not everything fits neatly into just two kingdoms. Now many scientists say there are five kingdoms.

From high in the air to deep in the ocean, scientists classify every creature.

## Orders, families, and genera

Scientists don't stop there. They divide all the birds into about 25 different groups, called orders. There is an order just of owls, one for penguins, one for woodpeckers, and so on. Orders are further divided into families. Families are divided into groups called **genera**. And each genus is divided into species. Every species is one particular kind of bird.

Let's take a look at just one bird and figure out which order it belongs to. This is the blue and yellow **macaw**.

Here are a few of the groups in the animal kingdom. Where does the macaw fit in? Which phylum, class, and order does it belong to?

| Animal Kingdom |
| --- |
| Phylum Echinodermata (These are the sea urchins and sand dollars.) |
| Phylum Annelida (These are earthworms.) |
| Phylum Arthropoda (This phylum includes insects and spiders.) |
| Phylum Chordata (These animals have a bundle of nerves down their backs, usually as a spinal cord.) |
|    Class Amphibia (These are frogs, toads, and salamanders.) |
|    Class Reptilia (These are lizards, turtles, and other animals with scales or plates.) |
|    Class Aves (These are songbirds, owls, and others that have feathers and lay eggs.) |
|       Order Passeriformes (These are songbirds, or small perching birds. On each foot they have three toes pointing forward, and one pointing back.) |
|       Order Piciformes (These are woodpeckers. They have two toes forward, and two toes back. They also have straight bills that they use to find food by pecking into trees.) |
|       Order Psittaciformes (This order includes parrots and cockatoos. They have strong, hooked bills, and are often brightly colored birds.) |
|       Order Strigiformes (These are the owls. They have strong bills and feet. Their eyes point forward.) |
|       Order Sphenisciformes (This order includes penguins. They cannot fly, but have webbed feet for swimming.) |
|    Class Mammalia (These are animals with hair.) |

# How Is a Bird Born?

Baby birds develop and grow inside eggs. Things are pretty crowded inside an egg. The baby bird shares space with the yolk, the "egg white," and **membranes**, including air space. The yolk provides food for the growing bird. As the baby grows larger, the yolk shrinks. The egg white, or **albumen**, provides water and protein. It surrounds the baby and protects it. The eggshell also protects the baby. It is hard, but it has hundreds of tiny holes, or pores, in it. The pores let air pass through the shell.

About the time the eggs are laid, many parent birds lose some of the feathers on their stomachs or sides. These bare spots are called brood patches. The parents rest these patches against their eggs to keep them warm.

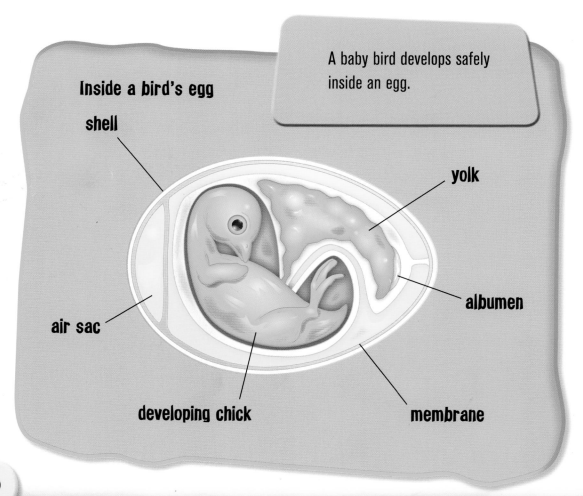

Inside a bird's egg

shell

yolk

albumen

air sac

developing chick

membrane

A baby bird develops safely inside an egg.

# Hatching

When a baby bird has used up all of the yolk, it is ready to hatch. Hatching is sometimes very slow. The little bird pecks and rests, pecks and rests, until it pecks its way out.

## Breaking Out!

The beak of a newborn bird has a very hard structure on its tip. It is called an egg tooth. It helps the baby peck its way out of the shell. In time, the little egg tooth falls off.

Some birds are born with no feathers at all. They are called **altricial** birds. They are born helpless and with their eyes closed. Robins and sparrows are altricial. Birds born with down feathers are called **precocial** birds. They start life with their eyes wide open. Ducks, quail, and turkeys are precocial birds.

# Types of feathers

As baby birds grow, they develop different kinds of feathers. Some birds, such as baby chickens and ducks, are born with short, soft feathers. These are called down feathers, and they keep the bird warm. In time, birds become covered by stiffer, longer feathers called **contour** feathers. These feathers give the bird its color and shape. Contour feathers of the wings and tail help birds to fly. Some birds also grow little "whiskers" around their beaks. These are not hairs but are tiny contour feathers.

These baby ducks are covered with down feathers.

# Parts of a feather

All feathers have a main stem called a shaft. Hairlike strands called barbs stick out from the shaft. On down feathers, the barbs are soft and loose. On contour feathers, they are stiff and stick together. How do they do this? Each barb has dozens of tiny **barbules**. These interlock with other barbules to keep the barbs stuck together.

Barbs stick out sideways from this feather's shaft. Tiny barbules stick out from the barbs. They interlock with nearby barbules.

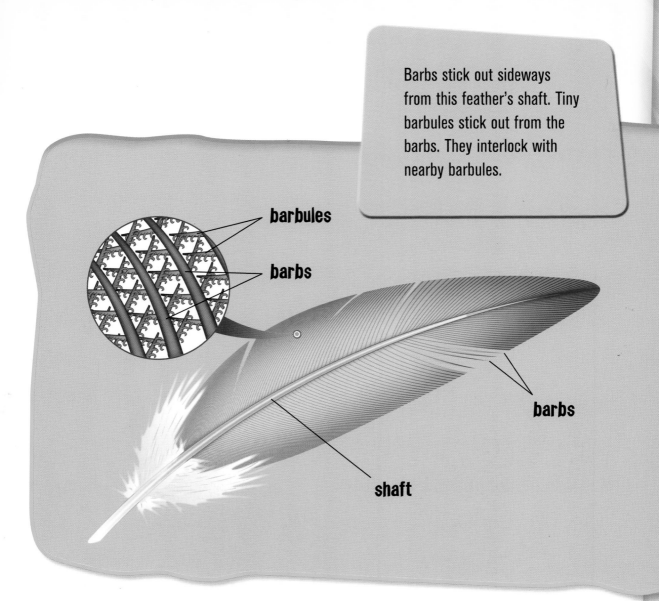

barbules

barbs

barbs

shaft

# How Does a Bird Grow?

Not long after birds hatch, they get hungry. Within days, **precocial** birds will leave the nest and begin finding their own food. Little ducklings follow their parents and pick up food. Young turkeys need a little more help. Their parents stop to show their babies which foods are good.

It's a different story with **altricial** birds. These babies are born with their eyes closed. They would have no hope of finding their own food. So right after they hatch, the parents begin feeding them in the nest. The adult birds may make hundreds of trips a day, finding food and bringing it back to the nest.

These babies are hungry! Their red, wide-open mouths signal the parent to put the food inside.

## Cleaning and protecting

Adult birds also work to keep the nest clean. They use their beaks to pick up little globs of their babies' waste. Then they fly away from the nest, dropping the globs at a distance. This helps keep the nest tidy. It also helps keep **predators** from finding the young birds.

### Milk from a Pigeon?

Some birds have developed a special way to feed their young. An organ in their chest produces a rich, nutritious liquid. The organ is called the crop, and the liquid is sometimes called crop milk. Pigeons and flamingos produce this food for their young.

# Ready to take off

Within weeks, both altricial and precocial birds will grow their **contour** feathers. At this point, the birds are called **fledglings**. These are birds that are about ready to fly. However, they are not quite prepared to take off. They need some practice.

Little fledglings in the nest may stand and flap their wings. This strengthens their chest and wing muscles. Young hawks may hop from the nest to nearby branches, flapping all the way. Vultures might jump and climb about on rocks while stretching their huge wings. These activities are preparing the birds for flight.

The speckles and streaks on this robin's chest show that it is still young. Later on, it will develop the reddish orange chest of an adult.

In this photo, you can see the adult robin's orange chest and the baby robins' speckled chests.

## Different looks

Although they have contour feathers, many young birds look nothing like their parents. Young robins have speckled chests, while the adult chests are solid orange. And a young bald eagle is almost solid brown. It does not have the white head and tail of the adult.

# How Do Birds Move?

Most birds are built for flying. Their bones, muscles, and nerves are all designed for this way of traveling.

Flying requires strong muscles in the chest, sides, shoulders, and wings. The largest muscle in flying birds runs from the chest to the upper arm. Birds use this muscle to pull their wings downward. They use another large muscle to pull their wings upward. Some muscles pull the birds' wings forward or tilt them during flight. Others twist or spread the tail for steering and slowing down.

Birds such as this African fish eagle need many strong muscles to be able to use their wings to fly.

# Bones built for flying

All flight muscles are attached to bones. In birds, certain bones are built specifically to handle these strong muscles. Like many other animals, birds have a sternum, or breastbone. The sternum in birds is very large and has a flat, bony portion sticking forward. This is called the keel. It provides plenty of attachment space for the flight muscles.

With all of this extra bony material, birds should be heavy. But this is not the case. Birds' bones are filled with air spaces. They are also strengthened inside by tiny **struts**. The spaces and struts make the bones lightweight, yet strong.

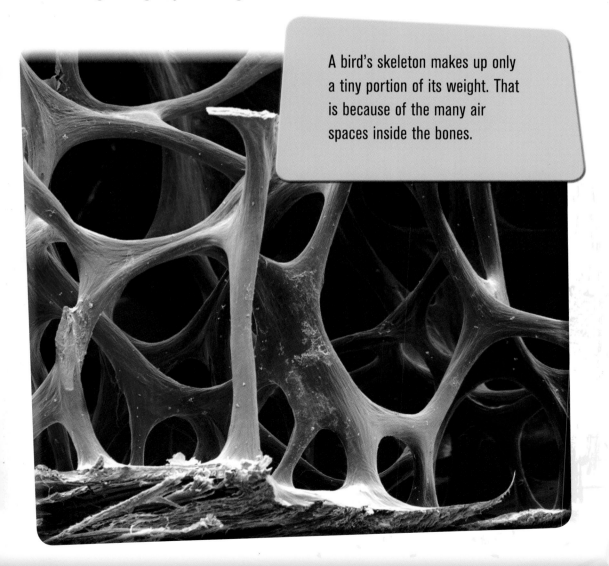

A bird's skeleton makes up only a tiny portion of its weight. That is because of the many air spaces inside the bones.

## Other ways to travel

Flying is not the only way that birds get around. They also hop, run, swim, climb, and glide. Ducks, geese, and gulls spend plenty of time in the water. Their feet are webbed for swimming. Mockingbirds, bluebirds, and other perching birds often hop along tree branches. Their feet have three toes in front and one in back. They are designed for clinging to tree limbs and keeping the birds balanced. Woodpeckers hop up the sides of trees. Their feet have two toes in front and two in back. This keeps the birds from falling backward.

This jacana feeds in lakes where there are floating plants. Its long toes allow it to step from plant to plant without sinking.

Sometimes it's just easier to slide than to walk.

## Stuck on the ground

Some birds cannot fly at all. These include ostriches, **emus**, **kiwis**, and penguins. Although they are flightless, they each have their own way of traveling. Ostriches, emus, and **rheas** are terrific runners. They have long legs and strong leg muscles. They do have wings. But they use them for steering and balance when running.

Penguins are master swimmers. Their bodies are streamlined so they easily slip through the water. Their wings work as flippers, and they use their feet and tails to steer. Penguins live where the oceans are very cold. Their thick layer of feathers and their body fat **insulate** them, or keep them warm, against the chilly waters.

# Time for a trip

Many birds stay in one area for their whole lives. They find plenty of food, water, and shelter right where they are. Other birds, however, make long trips every year. They do this for one main reason. They need to live and raise their chicks where there is plenty of food.

Most birds that live near the equator can find food all year long. Fruit, berries, seeds, insects, and fish are always available. Birds here do not need to leave. But far north and south of the equator, cold winters force the birds to look elsewhere. Many make long trips to find food. These trips are called **migrations**. Migrations are often long and difficult. Birds prepare by eating plenty of food before they start out, storing energy in their body fat.

### The Longest Trip

Arctic terns make the longest known migrations of any animal. Each year in August, the birds leave their far northern homes around Greenland and Iceland. They take about three months to reach Antarctica, where the water is rich with food. In April, they leave, heading north again. The entire trip covers about 70,000 kilometers (43,500 miles). In its lifetime, an arctic tern can travel the same distance as three trips to the Moon and back!

Migrating birds usually return to the same spots each year. Scientists have wondered how the birds know just where to go. After all, their trips may be hundreds of miles long. Now they believe the birds use the Sun and stars to guide them on their trips.

The tiny ruby-throated hummingbird fattens up before starting its migration.

# How Do Birds Protect Themselves?

Birds face all sorts of dangers during their lives. Some **predators** eat their eggs. Others go after their young or hunt the adults. So what can birds do to protect themselves?

## Camouflage

Some birds lay eggs that are **camouflaged**. These eggs have colors or markings that make them difficult to see. Egg-eating animals have trouble finding them. **Plovers** lay their eggs on the ground, often in sandy places. The eggs have dark speckles on a light-colored background. The common **murre** lays its eggs on high cliffs. The eggs are sharply pointed at one end. If something bumps these eggs, they don't roll off the cliff. Instead, they just roll in a circle!

Although these eggs are out in the open, they are still difficult for predators to see.

Adult birds also have tricks for protecting themselves. Bitterns live among **reeds** in marshy areas. These birds are streaked with brown and white markings. When they sense danger, these bitterns freeze in place with their heads pointed upward. They blend in perfectly with their surroundings.

## Huge size

Some birds simply rely on their size for protection. The Andean condor has a wingspan of 3 meters (10 feet). And the adult ostrich is taller than a refrigerator, and weighs more than a washing machine. Not many predators want to mess with those birds!

This bittern knows exactly how to hide from its enemies.

## Poison

Two birds are known to have their own method of protection. One is the little **pitohui** of Indonesia. It looks perfectly harmless. But its skin and feathers are loaded with poison. One taste is all it takes to keep enemies away!

## Acting

Many birds actively defend themselves. Camouflage and size just aren't enough for them. Some of these birds have tricks to defend their eggs. When the mother killdeer senses that her eggs are in danger, she actually flutters away from them. Then she goes into an act. She limps along the ground, holds a wing out, or spreads her tail to pretend she is injured. This is her way of drawing predators away from her eggs.

This mother bird is hoping to lure predators away from her eggs.

## "Don't mess with me"

Some birds try to scare intruders. Barn owls, for instance, will rock their heads back and forth, hiss, and snap their bills. Small birds often take it to the next level. When a large bird swoops too near to their nests, these small birds go into attack mode. They will zoom in to peck the larger bird and shoo it away.

### Calls and Songs

No matter where birds live, they always have ways to communicate with each other. Perching birds make two kinds of sounds—songs and calls. Songs are often musical and include several notes. Males use them to attract females. Calls, however, are short, and usually just one or two notes. These can be calls for help or warning, or to locate another bird. Young birds living in the nest use calls to ask for food. Some warning calls can be recognized by other **species** of birds or other animals.

Small birds will often attack larger ones in order to protect their nests and young.

# Where Do Birds Live?

Birds live on almost every landmass on Earth. Some are **adapted** to life near the water, while others are better suited for **inland** life.

Waterbirds have colors, body shapes, wings, bills, legs, and feet that are designed for **aquatic** life. Most gulls and terns are white underneath and black on the upper side of their wings. This helps them blend in with their environment. Penguins have round, bullet-shaped bodies that are perfect for swimming and diving. Like ducks, geese, and swans, they also have webbed feet that help them steer when swimming.

Wading birds such as herons and flamingos have long, slender legs. As they walk out from the shore and water swirls around them, they remain steady and do not fall over.

## Unusual beaks

Some ocean birds have unusual beaks for feeding. Pelicans use their huge bills to scoop up fish. Oystercatchers have long, strong beaks. They poke their bills between the shells of oysters and clams and clip their muscles. The animals cannot close their shells and the oystercatchers enjoy easy meals.

Many waterbirds have beaks for snagging fish. Kingfishers are small birds with big heads and long beaks. They perch on tree branches or power lines and stare down into lakes or ponds. When they see the glisten of a fish, they drop into a power dive and grab it.

With their spindly legs and long beaks, these spoonbills are clearly built for life near water. Spoonbills swish their long bills back and forth in shallow water, picking up shrimp, insects, and other small pieces of food.

## Other bird habitats

Not all birds live near the water. Many live in deserts, icy regions, fields, forests, and cities. Birds that live in extreme temperatures are terrific survivors. The little cactus wren lives in a hot, dry desert. It hides out in the shade during the heat of the day. It gets all of its water from the insects and fruit that it eats. The snowy owl and the **ptarmigan** live in the icy cold Arctic. Both have thick layers of feathers, even on their legs.

The elf owl is one of the smallest of all owls. It lives in the desert of the southwestern United States. It makes its home in abandoned woodpecker nests in cactus plants and trees.

Cliff swallows make their nests in all kinds of places. They build their nests under bridges and overpasses, and even on the sides of buildings.

Some birds have become adapted for life in unusual places. Cliff swallows live in canyons. They build their nests by packing mud balls onto the sides of cliffs. As cities grew, these swallows learned to build nests under bridges and on the sides of buildings. They changed as their environment changed.

Grassland birds find food and build their nests in hayfields and meadows. They are good at clinging to swaying **reeds**. Many, such as meadowlarks and cowbirds, have brown, black, or yellow markings. They blend in with their surroundings. Some hawks and owls also prefer grasslands, where they can fly over, hunting for mice or rabbits.

# How Do Birds Help Us?

Like all other animals, birds are **consumers**. They eat plants or other animals and help keep balance in nature. For example, purple **martins** and house martins eat insects. A single bird might eat hundreds of mosquitoes or flies in a day. This helps to keep these insect populations under control.

Birds that eat fruit and berries also help nature. Their droppings contain these plants' seeds. As birds travel about, they spread the seeds, so plants can grow in new places. In time, these new plants provide food for many other animals.

Birds such as this purple martin eat insects, helping keep the insect population under control.

Birds often become the food for other animals, including humans. But people also depend on them for other things. People keep parrots, parakeets, mynahs, and other small birds as pets. They wear jackets filled with goose down and sleep on feather pillows. And people have adorned clothing, hats, and jewelry with feathers for years. But that's not all. Gardeners use pigeon droppings on their plants. They say this waste makes outstanding **fertilizer**!

### Carolina Parakeet

Years ago, Carolina parakeets were common in the United States. But in the 1800s, farmers killed them to protect their crops. Hunters killed them for their feathers, which were used in women's hats. This went on for years. By the 1920s, not a single Carolina parakeet was left. This is a sad example of humans causing an animal to become **extinct**.

## Trouble in the skies

In some places, birds have created problems. They have destroyed crops, damaged airplanes, and spread disease. These problems, however, were probably not entirely the birds' fault.

One example is the European starling. At one time, these birds lived only in Europe, Asia, and northern Africa. But eventually, people brought them to the United States, Australia, and New Zealand. They hoped that the birds would do well in their new homes and would help destroy insect pests. As it turned out, the birds became pests themselves.

Starlings eat insects, fruit, seeds, and even table scraps. They can live in all types of environments, from forests to crowded cities. Sometimes thousands of them move into a new area at once. Then they simply take over. They eat insects that other birds need for food. They eat the feed that farmers put out for their livestock. They foul the food and water meant for cattle. They eat the fruit and grain crops they were meant to protect.

The European starling was brought to other continents in hopes that it would help control the insect population. Instead, the bird became a pest.

### Pretty and Pesky

Starlings are not the only problem birds. At one time, wealthy home owners in North America brought mute swans over from Europe and Asia. They enjoyed having these beautiful birds and watching their graceful movements. But the swans turned out to be troublesome. They attacked other **species**. They ate the plants that ducks and geese needed for food. Now, experts are working on ways to control these birds.

# How Do Birds Spend Their Time?

Birds spend most of their time resting, sleeping, and eating. Birds that look for food in the daytime are called **diurnal** birds. Those that hunt and feed at night are called **nocturnal** birds. Most owls are nocturnal hunters. Their outstanding hearing and eyesight help them find **prey** in the dark.

This flamingo really knows how to relax. As it sleeps, its breathing and heart rate slow down.

When birds are flying about and hunting, their breathing and heart rates speed up. Birds have two lungs, just like humans do. But they also have big air sacs connected to those lungs. All of these air sacs help birds get enough oxygen while in flight, especially at very high altitudes.

Birds do not have teeth but they swallow whole mouthfuls of food at a time. In some birds, the food then slides down the throat into a chamber called the crop. There, it begins to soften. Next, the food moves into a two-part stomach. The first part contains acid that breaks the food down. The second part is the gizzard, which grinds the food. From there, the food moves through the intestines. Here, the nutrients are drawn through the intestinal walls, so they can move out to the rest of the body.

### Do Birds Eat Rocks?

Muscles of the gizzard squeeze and relax, crushing food into small pieces. Tiny chunks of gravel in the gizzard help grind the food. But how does the gravel get there? The bird picks it up from the ground and swallows it!

# Grooming

Birds spend at least part of their day preening, or taking care of their feathers. This keeps their feathers in good shape for flying and swimming. Many birds have a structure called the preen gland. It is near the tail and produces oil. Birds rub their beaks over this gland to pick up the oil. Then they stroke it through their feathers. This keeps the feathers smooth, shiny, and waterproof.

This mallard duck is stroking oil from its preen gland through its feathers. Oil from the gland helps the bird to shed water.

Birds also keep their feathers clean by bathing and dusting. Bathing not only cleans the feathers and skin, but also helps birds to cool off in hot weather. Birds that live in dry areas clean themselves by dusting. They either find a good, dusty spot on the ground, or they make one by scraping their feet in the dirt. They wallow in the dust, sling it over their bodies, and rub their heads in it. Then they work it through their feathers before shaking it out.

### Birds Getting Antsy

Many birds keep themselves clean by a process called anting. Some pick up ants and poke them into their feathers. Others lie down on anthills, spreading their wings so ants can crawl over their bodies. Why would they do this? Ants produce chemicals that can kill germs and parasites. Scientists think that the ants release these chemicals as they move through the birds' feathers. This might keep the birds from getting skin diseases or parasites.

# How Do Birds Have Babies?

At the time of year when food is plentiful, birds prepare to have babies. First, the male birds begin looking for mates. This is a period called courtship, and males will do everything they can to attract females. In some **species**, the males sing. In others, they dance, show off their feathers, or prove what great nest builders they are.

Peafowl are champions at showing off. The males, or peacocks, spread their magnificent tail feathers and **strut** about, hoping to attract peahens.

This blue-footed booby is busy showing off his handsome feet in hopes of attracting a mate.

Bowerbirds of Australia take another approach. The males build complex homes, called bowers, on the forest floor. They use sticks, weeds, leaves, and moss to create enormous structures. Next, they decorate them with flowers, shells, feathers, and pebbles. Females come by to inspect the bowers. Once a female is satisfied with the work, the birds will mate. Then the female flies off to build a new nest for her eggs.

## Special nests for baby birds

Birds create nests specifically as homes for their young. Tiny birds such as hummingbirds build small, delicate, cup-shaped nests. Large birds such as eagles create enormous nests that weigh hundreds of pounds. Other birds weave saclike nests in trees or make simple nests of mud on the ground.

The weaver birds of Africa build nests that dangle from trees.

## The cycle begins again

Once the nest is ready, the female lays her eggs. Parents then keep the eggs warm until they are ready to hatch. For some woodpeckers, this **incubation** period lasts about a week and a half. For **albatrosses**, it can last almost three months!

At hatching, the life cycle begins again. The young grow up and leave the nest. Some die before they become adults. They become ill or are eaten by **predators**. However, many survive, and eventually have babies of their own. Some birds start a new family every year. Small birds such as house wrens might live and produce young for six or seven years. Larger birds such as geese, terns, and swans can do this into their twenties or even longer. As long as this cycle continues, the species will survive.

### That's Cuckoo!
European cuckoos are unusual birds. They are completely unable to care for their eggs and young. So how does this species survive? The female cuckoo lays an egg in the nest of another bird. Sometimes she even removes one of the eggs already in the nest. When the nesting mother returns, she may not notice the cuckoo egg, and warms it as if it were her own. When the young cuckoo hatches, it shoves all other eggs from the nest. It quickly becomes the center of attention with its adopted parents working hard to keep it fed.

All birds pass through this life cycle from egg to adult.

egg

nestling

fledgling

adult

courtship and mating

nesting

# Bird Facts

## What is the largest bird?

The ostrich is the largest living bird. Males can grow to be 2.7 meters (8.8 feet) tall and weigh as much as 130 kilograms (287 pounds).

## What is the smallest bird?

The bee hummingbird of Cuba is the smallest. The body of this tiny bird weighs less than a marble.

## What is the fastest bird?

The peregrine falcon can fly at a speed of almost 145 kilometers (90 miles) per hour. When diving at **prey**, this bird zooms at almost 322 kilometers (200 miles) per hour.

## Which birds build the most unusual nests?

Several birds are the winners here. Bald eagles add sticks to their nests every year. Over time, these nests can come to weigh more than one ton! The **pied-billed grebe** builds a floating nest hidden among **reeds** in the water. And small **swifts** in Asia build their nests entirely out of saliva!

# Bird classification

Scientists divide birds into about 25 different orders. The perching birds form the largest order. More than half of all bird **species** fit into this group.

Orders with several hundred species include the hummingbirds, woodpeckers, gulls, parrots, pigeons and doves, and the hawks and eagles. Orders with less than 200 species include the owls, cuckoos, herons, pelicans, and penguins.

Scientists place this **kiwi** in the same group as the ostrich. Can you guess why?

# Glossary

**adapt** to adjust to new or different conditions

**albatross** large seabird with webbed feet

**albumen** clear, jellylike part of an egg

**altricial** helpless when born

**ancient** extremely old

**aquatic** living in or near water, or dealing with water

**Archaeopteryx** genus name of an extinct bird

**Aves** class within the animal kingdom that includes all of the birds

**barbule** small extension from the barbs on contour feathers

**camouflage** having colors or patterns that make something difficult to see

**classification** method of organizing things

**consumer** living thing that eats plants or animals

**contour** shape of something

**diurnal** active mainly during the daytime

**emu** large, flightless bird similar to the ostrich

**extinct** having died out

**fertilizer** material that adds nutrients to the soil

**fledgling** young bird that has just grown its flight feathers

**fossil** remains of a plant or animal that died long ago

**genus (pl. genera)** group into which plants and animals are classified

**incubation** warming of eggs, usually by sitting on them, before the eggs hatch

**inland** away from coasts and shorelines

**insulate** to be protected from the loss of heat

**kiwi** flightless bird of New Zealand

**macaw** large, long-tailed parrot

**martin** slender, insect-eating bird

**membrane** very thin sheet of tissue lining the inside of an egg

**migration** trip made by animals, usually every year, to find food

**murre** black and white diving bird

**nocturnal** active mainly at night

**phylum** one of the major groups within the animal kingdom

**pied-billed grebe** small diving bird that lives on lakes and ponds of North America

**pitohui** New Guinea bird that is one of two known poisonous birds

**plover** small shorebird with long legs

**precocial** active at birth, and needing little care from parents

**predator** animal that hunts and eats other animals

**prey** animal that is eaten by other animals

**ptarmigan** chicken-like bird that lives in cold areas

**reed** stalk of a tall grass plant

**rhea** large, flightless bird similar to an ostrich

**species** particular kind of living thing

**strut** brace or support that strengthens a structure; way of walking

**swift** small bird with slender wings

**vertebrate** animal with a backbone

# Find Out More

## Books

Bradley, James V. *Crows and Ravens (Nature Walk)*. New York: Chelsea Clubhouse, 2006.

Burnie, David. *Bird*. New York: DK, 2008.

Facts on File. *The Encyclopedia of Birds*. New York: Infobase, 2007.

Osborne, Mary Pope, and Natalie Pope Boyce. *Penguins and Antarctica (Magic Tree House Research Guide)*. New York: Random House, 2008.

## Websites

The Great Backyard Bird Count
www.birdsource.org/gbbc/kids/gbbc-is-for-kids

The Life of Birds
www.pbs.org/lifeofbirds/

National Geographic Kids: Creature Features
http://kids.nationalgeographic.com/kids/animals/creaturefeature

Smithsonian National Zoological Park: Birds
http://nationalzoo.si.edu/Animals/Birds/ForKids/default.cfm

# Index